P9-DFR-320

POINT OF IMPACT

Assassination in Sarajevo

The Trigger for World War I

STEWART ROSS

Heinemann Library
Chicago, Illinois

© 2001 Reed Educational & Professional Publishing
Published by Heinemann Library,
an imprint of Reed Educational & Professional Publishing,
Chicago, IL

Customer Service 888-454-2279

Visit our website at www.heinemannlibrary.com

All rights reserved. No part of this publication may be reproduced or transmitted in any form or by any means, electronic or mechanical, including photocopying, recording, taping, or any information storage and retrieval system, without permission in writing from the publisher.

Produced for Heinemann Library by Discovery Books Limited
Designed by Ian Winton
Illustrations by Stefan Chabluk
Printed in Hong Kong

05 04 03 02
10 9 8 7 6 5 4 3 2

Library of Congress Cataloging-in-Publication Data

Ross, Stewart.
    Assassination at Sarajevo : the trigger for World War One / Stewart Ross.
        p. cm. -- (Point of impact)
    Includes bibliographical references and index.
    ISBN 1-58810-074-X (library binding)
    1. World War, 1914-1918--Causes--Juvenile literature. 2. Franz Ferdinand,
Archduke of Austria, 1863-1914--Assassination--Juvenile literature. [1. World War,
1914-1918--Causes. 2. Franz Ferdinand, Archduke of Austria,
1863-1914--Assassination.] I. Title. II. Series.

D512 .R67 2001
904.3'11--dc21
                                00-046094

Acknowledgments
The Publishers would like to thank the following for permission to reproduce photographs:
Hulton Getty, pp. 4, 5, 8, 16, 21, 25; Mary Evans, front cover top, pp. 7, 9, 10, 12, 13, 14, 17, 19, 20, 26; Popperfoto, pp. 11, 17, 22 (front cover bottom); Peter Newark's Military Pictures, p. 15; Imperial War Museum, p. 18; Camera Press, p. 23; Peter Newark's Historical Pictures, pp. 24, 27; Corbis/Michael St. Maur Sheil, p. 29.

Cover photographs reproduced with permission of Mary Evans and Popperfoto.

Every effort has been made to contact copyright holders of any material reproduced in this book. Any omissions will be rectified in subsequent printings if notice is given to the Publisher.

Some words are shown in bold, **like this.** You can find out what they mean by looking in the glossary.

Contents

Assassination!

Two fatal shots

It was Sunday, June 28, 1914, in Sarajevo, Bosnia. Beside Schiller's café, on the corner of Franz Joseph Street, a young man gazed miserably across the road. What should he do? His colleagues had failed in their **assassination** attempt, and the archduke had escaped. Now the police hunt was on. . . .

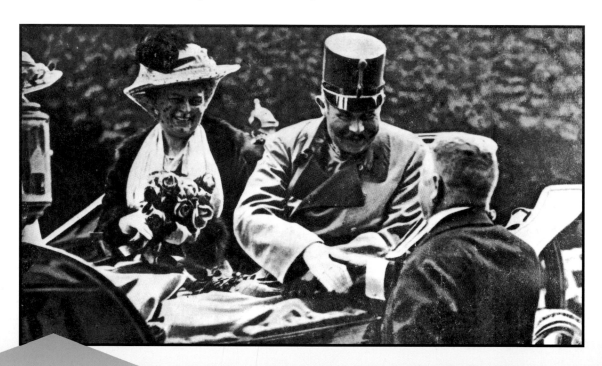

Archduke Franz Ferdinand and his wife, Sophie, were photographed in Sarajevo shortly before they were shot dead by an assassin.

Suddenly, a large open car rounded the corner, stopped, and began to back up. It was the archduke and his party! The young assassin had his opportunity. Without hesitating, he pulled out his gun, stepped forward, and fired two shots. The first hit the archduke in the neck. The second ricocheted into his wife's stomach. Both wounds were fatal. This assassination was the trigger for a war that soon engulfed much of the world.

What happened next?

Archduke Franz Ferdinand was heir to the throne of Austria-Hungary, a mighty European power. The government of Austria-Hungary blamed Serbia for his death and declared war. Although a small country, Serbia had a powerful friend in Russia. So when Serbia was attacked, the Russians entered the conflict. The **allies** of Austria-Hungary and Russia were drawn in, spreading the war across Europe and beyond.

One small mistake

By the time the U. S. became involved in 1917, the squabble between Austria-Hungary and Serbia had grown into a terrible world war. Was anyone to blame, or was it just a series of dreadful accidents? The assassin shot Franz Ferdinand when the archduke's car took a wrong turn. Had one small mistake by the driver changed the history of the world?

ASSASSINATION IN HISTORY

The word *assassination* means "a political murder." Throughout history, many political leaders have been assassinated.

Here are some other well-known assassinations:

44 B.C.E. Julius Caesar was stabbed to death by a group of his fellow Romans.

1763 French revolutionary leader Jean-Paul Marat was stabbed to death by Charlotte Corday while he was taking a bath.

1865 U.S. president Abraham Lincoln was shot dead by John Wilkes Booth, an actor.

1963 U.S. president John F. Kennedy was shot dead by sniper Lee Harvey Oswald in Dallas, Texas.

1984 Indian prime minister Indira Gandhi was murdered by her own bodyguards.

1995 Israeli prime minister Yitzhak Rabin was shot dead at a peace rally by a Jewish extremist.

The shattered French town of Verdun lay on the front line between the French and German armies during World War I. Could all this devastation have resulted from two small pistol shots in Sarajevo?

To Die for Your Country

The nation-state

There are over 200 **nation-states** in today's world. These are self-governing countries in which the majority of the people speak the same language and share a common culture and history. In 1914, the idea of a nation-state was quite new to most people. Only in the 1860s, for example, had the separate states and cities of Italy been united into a single nation-state. A similar process took place in Germany at about the same time. Serbia was a new country, too. Before 1878 it had been a province of the Ottoman **Empire.**

Nationalism

The peoples of the new states and the older ones, such as Britain and France, were passionately proud

This is a map of Europe in the year 1914.

of their countries. This pride is known as "nationalism." Nationalists paid great respect to their country's symbols, such as its national anthem and flag. Children were taught at school to love their country. Newspapers, popular songs, and poems all helped increase nationalist feelings.

LAND OF HOPE AND GLORY

A. C. Benson's famous lines in praise of Britain, written in 1902, are a good example of nationalist feelings common at the time.

"Land of Hope and Glory, Mother of the Free,
How shall we extol thee who are born of thee?
Wider still and wider shall thy bounds be set;
God who made thee mighty, make thee mightier yet."

Wars of independence

Nationalism helped to bind a country together, but it also had its dangers. It could lead people to believe that war was a glorious thing. Extreme nationalists believed that it was noble to fight—even to die—for one's country.

Nationalism also inspired people to fight for their country's independence from foreign powers. The Serbs, for example, had been part of the Ottoman Empire since 1459. In 1876, they began a bloody war for independence. They were successful, and in 1878 the Ottomans recognized Serbia as an independent nation-state.

Serbian women as well as men underwent military training in 1908 as the Serbian nation prepared to defend itself.

The Ottoman Empire

The age of empire

In the early 20th century, much of the world was divided into **empires.** An empire was created when one nation-state with a strong government took control of other countries. The British Empire, by far the largest, stretched right around the globe. France, the Netherlands, Portugal, and Germany also had overseas empires. In and around Europe lay three ancient empires: the Russian Empire, the Turkish (or Ottoman) Empire, and the Austro-Hungarian (or Hapsburg) Empire.

Empires occurred because of the natural tendency of the strong to control the weak. The "mother country"—the controlling government—often exploited its colonies. Subject nations provided natural resources, labor, and various other benefits to the mother country.

Celebrations such as this 1913 Empire Day at a British school helped teach nationalism.

One way to keep an empire strong was to have many colonies. Another way was to weaken other empires by depriving them of their colonies. This formula was to figure into events at the turn of the century.

Imperial families

Some 19th century empires, like the British and the French, were governed by elected **ministers** and their agents. Other empires, like the Russian and the Austro-Hungarian, were governed by hereditary rulers, as kingdoms were passed from father to son. The Austro-Hungarian Empire, for instance, was also known as the Hapsburg Empire because it was ruled by Austria's **hereditary** ruling family, the Hapsburgs.

Imperialism versus nationalism

The imperial powers were eager to increase the size of their empires. This spirit of empire-building is known as imperialism. Clearly, imperialism clashed head-on with nationalism, which inspired peoples to break away from imperial rule. In some regions the clash between imperialism and nationalism had serious consequences.

The sick man

In the 17th century, the Ottoman Turks had controlled a huge empire in eastern Europe and the Middle East. Over time, however, this empire had become weak and started to crumble. Its rulers failed to adopt new ideas in technology and government. By the late 19th century, the Ottoman Empire was known as the "sick man of Europe." Few believed it would recover.

The vultures gather

Some peoples of the Ottoman Empire, like the Greeks and Serbs, had broken away to become independent **nation-states.** Other lands had been taken over by neighboring empires. Like vultures, the imperial powers hovered over the "sick man" to see what else they could seize.

Ottoman ruler Abdul Hamid II was unable to stop his empire from being torn apart. This French cartoon of 1908 shows Bulgaria declaring itself independent while Austria-Hungary seizes Bosnia and Herzegovina.

Le Petit Journal

Le Petit Journal   **5** CENTIMES   SUPPLÉMENT ILLUSTRÉ   **5** CENTIMES   ABONNEMENTS

DIMANCHE 18 OCTOBRE 1908

LE REVEIL DE LA QUESTION D'ORIENT
La Bulgarie proclame son indépendance. — L'Autriche prend la Bosnie et l'Herzégovine

The Powder Keg

The Balkans

The Balkans were home to a broad mix of peoples. The work "Balkans" comes from the Turkish word for mountains, and in this mountainous region lived Macedonians, Greeks, Albanians, Serbs, Croats, Bosnians, Bulgarians, and Romanians. In some areas, such as Bosnia, several peoples lived alongside each other. There were also two major religions in the Balkans: Christianity and Islam. These cultural and religious differences made the region very unstable.

Imperial rivalry

The Balkans lie at the crossroads between Europe and the Middle East. Here the frontiers of the Ottoman, Austro-Hungarian, and Russian **Empires** met. The British also had a strong interest in the area. They did not want it to fall into the hands of a rival power. If this happened, the route through the Suez Canal to India, one of the British Empire's most profitable colonies, would be threatened. In 1878, Russia and Turkey went to war. To keep Russia out of the Balkans, Britain threatened to join the war on Turkey's side, and so peace was made at the **Congress** of Berlin.

As shown in this 1912 French magazine illustration, the breakup of the Ottoman Empire turned many Turkish people in the Balkans into refugees.

Agreement for peace

Despite the Berlin agreement, by 1900, the Turks had been largely driven out of the Balkans. No imperial power had taken over after them, and the region split into small **nation-states.** There was much rivalry between them, causing the area to be known as the "powder keg of Europe." In 1903, worried that the area might erupt into violence, Russia and Austria-Hungary agreed to cooperate to keep the peace.

Conflicts in the Balkans have yet to be resolved. This 1999 picture shows the devastation caused by the recent troubles in Kosovo, a province of Serbia populated mostly by Albanian Muslims. Although the Serbs seized Kosovo from the Turks in 1913, the Kosovar Albanians were never happy to be part of Serbia.

FANATICAL HATRED

"We are struck by the feelings of dislike and bitterness which Christians and Mahommedans [Muslims] feel for each other. There is no other district where the loathing between the [Christian] Cross and the [Muslim] Crescent is so strong."
A report to the Austro-Hungarian government on the conditions in Bosnia, 1875.

Serbia's Advance

Bosnia and Herzegovina

The 1878 **Congress** of Berlin had agreed that the Austrians could look after the twin provinces of Bosnia and Herzegovina. This arrangement annoyed Serbia because a large number of Serbs lived there. Indeed, the Serbian government sometimes felt that Bosnia and Herzegovina would be better off as part of Serbia.

Aehrenthal's move

For a long time, the government of Austria-Hungary had been worried by the growth of nationalism in the Balkans. It feared that nationalism would spread into their **empire** and break it up. So, in 1908, the new Austro-Hungarian foreign **minister,** Count Aehrenthal, decided to make a show of strength. He announced that Austria-Hungary was taking over Bosnia and Herzegovina completely and making them part of its empire.

The Austro-Hungarian empire's **annexation** of Herzegovina and Bosnia in 1908, under the leadership of Austrian Emperor Franz Joseph I (1830–1916), raised Serbian fears that they would be next.

12

RUSSIA'S MISSION

Many Russians believed they had a "mission" to look after their fellow Christians in the Balkans.

"Russia's historical mission was the freeing of the Christian peoples of the Balkans from the Turkish yoke. This was almost done by the beginning of the 20th century. Nevertheless, the young Balkan countries still needed Russia's help if anyone threatened them." [Serge Sazonov, Russia's foreign minister, 1928]

Nicholas II (1868–1918) was the last **tsar** of Russia. Weak and incompetent, he allowed Russia to be drawn into a war for which it was totally unprepared.

Fury and fear

The Serbs were furious when they heard of Aehrenthal's action. They were also frightened. Perhaps they would be next to be taken over. The Russians also were outraged, due to their close ties to the Serbs. They were both Slavic peoples who shared the same Orthodox form of Christianity. However, for now, the Russians backed away from direct confrontation with the Austro-Hungarians.

Russia's revenge

To show they still had influence in the region, the Russians encouraged the Serbs to go to war (1912–13). First the Serbs and their **allies** crushed the Turks, then they turned on Bulgaria. Their victories left Serbia bigger and stronger than ever. They also left Austria-Hungary believing that Serbia was a problem they would have to deal with sooner rather than later.

Beyond the Balkans

Alliances for strength and peace

By 1914, the great European powers were divided into two groups. In 1879, Austria-Hungary and Germany had signed a Dual Alliance. This said they would help each other if they were attacked. Italy joined this alliance, making it a Triple Alliance, in 1882.

The Triple Alliance left France feeling isolated. So, in 1894, it formed its own Dual Alliance with Russia. For several years Britain remained outside this system of alliances. But it too began to feel isolated and, in 1902, signed an alliance with Japan. This was followed, in 1904, with an **Entente** Cordiale ("friendly understanding") with France. Three years later, Britain signed a similar entente with Russia. This three-way alliance was called the Triple Entente.

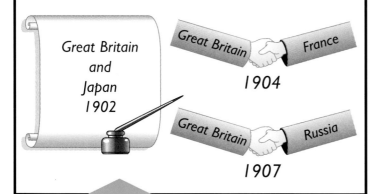

Triple Alliance

Germany and Austria-Hungary 1879 Joined by Italy 1882

Dual Alliance

France and Russia 1894

British Alliance and Ententes

Great Britain and Japan 1902

Great Britain — France 1904

Great Britain — Russia 1907

In the pre-war years, important alliances and ententes were made. Their purpose was to keep the balance of power within Europe.

One world

These alliances and ententes were supposed to prevent war by balancing one side (the Triple Alliance) against the other (the Triple Entente). But they also meant that events in the Balkans affected Europe and beyond. What concerned Russia, for example, also concerned its **ally,** France. Furthermore, because of Europe's **empires,** European events affected people worldwide. France's actions, for instance, affected its colonies from Indochina in Asia to North Africa.

Crisis and arms

The alliance system was tested by three serious European **crises** in the early 20th century. In 1905 and 1911, Germany challenged France's right to control Morocco. On both occasions Britain and Russia stood by France and the Germans backed down. However, in 1908, Russia had been the one to back down when Austria-Hungary took over Bosnia and Herzegovina.

After the 1911 showdown, it looked as if the alliance system was working. But the European war machines continued to grow: larger armies, newer weapons, and bigger fleets. What was all of this for if not for war? Would Germany or Russia be willing to back down again?

"EXPENSIVE LUXURY"

Throughout the 19th century, Britain's Royal Navy ruled the seas. Then, in the 1890s, Germany began building up a powerful navy of its own. British politicians said this was unnecessary (Winston Churchill called it "an expensive luxury") and feared it would be used to attack the British Empire. In response, Britain increased the power of the Royal Navy. When Germany did the same, an expensive "naval race" began.

Britain's revolutionary new battleship HMS *Dreadnought* was launched in 1906. Its high speed and huge guns set in revolving turrets rendered all other battleships obsolete. This forced the Germans to build stronger and larger ships of their own, fueling a costly naval race.

The Visit to Bosnia

The Emperor and his nephew

The Austro-Hungarian **Empire** was ruled by the ancient Hapsburg family. On the throne in 1914 was the narrow-minded and unsmiling Emperor Franz Joseph I. He knew all about the dangers of being a public figure—his wife had been **assassinated** in 1898. Archduke Franz Ferdinand, the heir to the throne, was Franz Joseph's nephew. He was a cold, hard man, but he was utterly devoted to his Czech wife, Sophie.

The archduke's plans

Franz Ferdinand understood that many of the emperor's subjects in the Austro-Hungarian empire wanted to leave and set up their own independent states. He knew, too, that the Serbs living in Bosnia were among the leaders of this movement. To keep them quiet, he planned to give them a greater say in their own government.

Archduke Franz Ferdinand is shown here with his family. His Czech wife, Sophie, was extremely unpopular in Austria.

THE BATTLE OF KOSOVO POLJE

Briefly, during the 14th century, the Serbs ruled a Christian empire that covered most of the Balkans. But on June 28 (St. Vitus's Day), 1389, the invading Muslim Turks defeated them at the Battle of Kosovo Polje. Although a disaster, the heroic feats of that day have inspired Serbian nationalists ever since.

Terrorist territory

In the summer of 1914, Franz Ferdinand went to Bosnia to watch the Austrian army training there. At the end of June, he planned a state visit to the important town of Sarajevo. He wanted to impress the citizens and show that he cared about them.

The visit was brave but unwise. Sarajevo was only 50 miles from the border with Serbia, and nationalist **terrorists** were known to operate there. The date of his visit, June 28, was not well chosen, either. It was the anniversary of the Battle of Kosovo Polje, one of the most significant events in Serbian history.

This is a picture of Sarajevo in 1893. The assassination took place just off the broad street that is visible to the right of the river in the top center of the picture.

Two Fatal Shots

The Black Hand

Before Franz Ferdinand's visit, Serbian **terrorists** had **assassinated** several Austro-Hungarian officials. When Danilo Ilic, the Sarajevo agent of the Black Hand terrorist gang, heard of the archduke's visit, he signed up six young men and instructed them in assassination techniques. One of his recruits was Gavrilo Princip.

Bomb attack

On Sunday, June 28, Franz Ferdinand and his **entourage** arrived at Sarajevo by train. At around 10:00 A.M. they left for the town hall in a procession of four cars. As they passed along the Appel Quay beside the river, one of Ilic's young accomplices hurled a bomb at the archduke's car.

Gavrilo Princip fired the two shots that killed the royal couple. He is shown here (far right) with two other members of the Black Hand Secret Society.

The archduke's bravery

Showing great bravery, the archduke managed to throw the bomb away before it exploded. Unfortunately, it went off beneath the car behind him, injuring several people. The procession now accelerated away towards the town hall. When he arrived, Franz Ferdinand declared angrily, *"So you welcome your guests here with bombs."* Then he asked to be taken to visit the injured.

Assassination

The route to the hospital was not properly explained to the archduke's driver. He took a wrong turn into Franz Joseph Street. Having heard the news of the failed bomb attack, Gavrilo Princip had left his post and was now standing, quite by chance, outside Schiller's café. He recognized the archduke's car at once. The moment it stopped, he advanced and fired the two fatal shots at close range. Franz Ferdinand and his wife died in a hospital fifteen minutes later.

This illustration provides a contemporary, although rather inaccurate, impression of the Sarajevo assassination. Sophie was hit by a stray bullet intended for one of her husband's generals.

GAVRILO PRINCIP

Nineteen-year-old Gavrilo Princip was a member of the "Young Bosnia" nationalist movement and was fanatically anti-Austrian. After the assassination he took poison. It did not work, however, and he was arrested. Too young to be hanged, he was kept in an Austrian jail until he died of tuberculosis four years later.

The Ultimatum

Deadly evidence

Although Princip and the other **terrorists** were Bosnians, their weapons were Serbian. Moreover, several important Serbian officials had known about the **assassination** plot and done nothing. Armed with this evidence, the Austro-Hungarian government decided to strike back.

German backing

The Austro-Hungarians did not attack Serbia right away for fear of Russia coming to Serbia's aid. They first turned to their major **ally,** Germany, for backing. Germany, still smarting from two showdowns with the French-British-Russian alliance, was perhaps less willing to back away from confrontation. Also, many in the German government believed that a European war was inevitable. They were also worried about Russia growing stronger. Deciding their chances for victory would be greater if they struck first, they gave Austria-Hungary their full support.

Kaiser Wilhelm II, after being advised by his staff, believed Germany's best hope of victory against France and Russia was to strike first—and fast.

The blank check

On July 5, 1914, the Austrian **ambassador** in Germany explained the "blank check" of support the Kaiser promised to give Austria-Hungary against Serbia: *"The Kaiser said . . . we might in this case . . . rely upon Germany's full support . . . It was the Kaiser's opinion that this action* [against Serbia] *must not be delayed."*

Accept, or else . . .

The Austro-Hungarian government still did not go to war. Instead, they sent the Serbs a ten-point **ultimatum.** This said they would invade if the Serbs did not give Austria-Hungary complete control over their country. They gave the Serbs just two days to send a reply.

War

The Serbian government accepted eight of the ultimatum's points but refused to accept Austrian officers in the Serbian army or Austrian **ministers** in the Serbian government. This was not good enough for Austria-Hungary and on July 29, it declared war on Serbia.

As Russians prepare for war, the infantry exercises with fixed bayonets. The enormous Russian army was seen by many as a "steamroller"—slow to start but unstoppable once it had got moving. The image did not take into account the deadly effect of machine guns.

Over by Christmas?

From Sarajevo to world war

When Serbia was attacked, Russia began to **mobilize** its forces against Austria-Hungary. In response, on August 1, Germany mobilized its forces and declared war on Russia. France, Russia's **ally,** began preparing for war. Eager to strike first, Germany then went to war with France. When German troops moved into **neutral** Belgium on August 4, Britain declared war on Germany.

Inspired by feelings of nationalism, millions on either side rushed to join the army. They believed the war would be over by Christmas and they did not want to miss it. They were tragically mistaken. Neither side managed to get the upper hand, and other nations were drawn into the conflict. By Christmas 1915, Turkey, Italy, and Bulgaria had entered the war. The United States, threatened by German aggression, finally joined in April 1917. The European war became the first-ever world war.

This photograph shows British troops going "over the top" during the Battle of the Somme in 1916. Ordered to walk calmly toward enemy lines, 60,000 men were killed or wounded in the first day's attack.

The two sides in World War I	
ALLIED POWERS	**CENTRAL POWERS**
France	Germany
Britain	Austria-Hungary
Russia	Ottoman Empire
Italy	Bulgaria
United States	
Serbia	
Montenegro	
Romania	
Greece	
Portugal	
Japan	
Brazil	

War of attrition

The war dragged on until November 1918. This was partly because, before the entry of the United States, the two sides were equally matched. Another reason was that defensive weapons were superior to attack weapons. Machine guns, barbed wire, and trenches made it almost impossible for foot soldiers to attack successfully. The result was a horrible war of **attrition** as each side tried to wear the other down.

Total war

The war produced horror on a scale never seen before. The numbers of people killed and wounded were enormous, and the hardships endured by soldiers living and fighting in cramped and filthy trenches were unspeakable. Moreover, the conflict affected everyone, soldiers and **civilians** alike. Millions of people were **conscripted** into the armed forces and other war work. In Europe, food was **rationed** and all available industry was geared toward winning the **"total war."** In the United States, families took part in voluntary conservation programs so that food could be sent to the Allies.

Breakthrough

At the end of 1917, a bloody **revolution** caused Russia to withdraw from the war. Germany's forces could now concentrate on fighting Britain, France, and the United States. By then, years of war had taken their toll on all the nations involved.

In the end, Germany was defeated because it was overwhelmed. A naval blockade prevented Germany from importing food and raw materials. American forces, backed by new offensive weapons—the airplane and the tank—finally gave the Allies (principally Britain, France, and the United States) sufficient power to force the Germans to surrender.

Italian soldiers carry a wounded comrade to safety after the Battle of Gorizia in 1916. Despite joining Germany and Austria-Hungary in the Triple Alliance in 1882, Italy entered the war on the side of the Allies in 1915.

The Lost Generation

Casualties

It is estimated that the war killed 1.8 million German soldiers and wounded 4.2 million more. The figures for Russia are 1.7 million killed and almost 5 million wounded. For France they are 1.38 million killed and 4.2 million wounded, and for the British Empire 950,000 and 2.1 million. In contrast, the United States suffered fewer than half a million killed and wounded.

Many of those killed in the fighting were young volunteers with their whole lives ahead of them. When they did not return home, their families spoke of them as the "lost generation."

Pacifism

During and after the war, an outbreak of influenza killed as many people as the fighting. Europe was shattered and demoralized. In the late 1920s, a stream of anti-war novels and poems appeared, including Erich Remarque's *All Quiet on the Western Front* (1929). Some who grew up in this postwar world were **pacifists** who believed all war was wrong.

British women voted in a general election for the first time in 1918. The right to vote was seen as a kind of reward for the vital work millions of women had done during the war.

Women prove a point

Only a few females had taken part in the fighting during the war. However, millions of women suffered when their countries were invaded or when they lost their fathers, brothers, husbands, and sons.

In one way, the war actually helped women. With most young men absent on the battlefield, women successfully took over men's jobs. This helped change attitudes toward women's rights. Between 1914 and 1939, women won the right to vote in 28 countries worldwide.

THE WAR POETS

Soldiers who openly criticized what was going on during the war risked being shot as cowards or traitors. However, some expressed their private feelings of disgust in poetry. One of these was British officer Siegfried Sassoon.

Suicide in the Trenches
I knew a simple soldier boy
Who grinned at life in empty joy,
Slept soundly through the lonesome dark,
And whistled early with the lark.

In winter trenches, cowed and glum,
With crumps and lice and lack of rum,
He put a bullet through his brain.
No one spoke of him again.

You smug-faced crowds with kindling eye
Who cheer when soldier lads march by,
Sneak home and pray you'll never know
The hell where youth and laughter go.

Siegfried Sassoon, 1918

Wilfred Owen, war poet and friend of Seigfried Sassoon (who survived the war), was killed just one week before the Armistice was signed. His vivid, realistic poems, published after his death, were influential in changing people's attitudes toward war.

A War to End All Wars?

The empires collapse

Many governments collapsed under the strain of **total war.** When the fighting went against them, the European **empires** of Russia, Turkey, Austria-Hungary, and Germany crumbled. Britain and France were exhausted and almost **bankrupt.** By contrast, the war left the United States the wealthiest and most powerful nation on Earth. As a result, the postwar world was quite different from the world that had gone to war so confidently in 1914.

Revolution in Russia

The **revolution** early in 1917 replaced Russia's ruler, the **tsar,** with a Western-style government. The new government briefly continued the war, leading to a second revolution in the autumn. This brought to power the world's first **Communist** government. The Communists executed the tsar and remained in power in Russia for over 70 years.

New states

The victorious **Allies** held a series of conferences to sort out postwar Europe. They divided the Austro-Hungarian and Ottoman Empires into **nation-states.** Austria and Hungary, for example, became separate countries. The small Balkan states, including Serbia and Bosnia, were formed into the new country of Yugoslavia.

This cartoon depicts Tsar Nicholas II giving up his throne in 1917 after having lost the respect of most of Russian society. His path to disgrace is lined by the ghosts of countless dead Russian soldiers. It is doubly ominous, for Nicholas and his family later were murdered by the revolutionary Communist government.

The victors decided Germany's fate at the Versailles Conference in 1919. They blamed it for causing the war, reduced it in size, took away its overseas colonies, and ordered it to pay $33 billion to the victors in compensation.

The new world

The Allies announced that the war had been "the war to end all wars." They hoped to avoid future conflicts by punishing their defeated enemies and setting up the **League of Nations** as a forum for peaceful debate. Neither policy worked. The League had no power to stop aggression. Many Germans deeply resented the harsh punishment. Some dreamed of revenge. In 1933, they chose a leader who promised them that revenge: Adolf Hitler.

GERMANY'S FAULT?

The **Treaty** drawn up by the Versailles Peace Conference blamed Germany for starting the war. The Germans were forced to accept this blame.

"Germany and her allies accept responsibility for causing all the Allies' wartime loss and damage, which came about as a result of the war brought upon them by the aggression of Germany and her allies."

[From the Treaty of Versailles, simplified]

Hitler's Nazi followers, called "brownshirts" are shown here at a rally in 1933. Hitler's popularity stemmed partly from his promise to restore German pride after suffering the humiliation of defeat and the effects of the harsh Treaty of Versailles.

Causes and Blame

What if?

Historians are interested in events, their causes, and their consequences. Asking "what if?" is not really their job. But it can sometimes help us understand why something happened. For example, what if Princip had missed the Archduke? Or what if the driver had not taken a wrong turn? Could the first world war have been avoided?

This map shows Europe after World War I.

Just one spark

Some people believe tiny events, like the driver's mistake, can have enormous consequences. Others believe small incidents have little influence. They point out, for instance, that for years Europe had been talking about war and preparing for it. It needed only a spark to set it off. That spark happened to be the **assassination.** But perhaps it could just as easily have been something else.

Whose fault?

Historians, like politicians, have tried to find someone to blame for World War I. Recently, they have pointed the finger at the Kaiser's government for offering unlimited support to Austria-Hungary. This was certainly unwise. But so were many other things, such as the **ultimatum,** Russia's **mobilization,** and the arms race in which all countries took part.

Though the causes of the war were very complicated, what we do know for certain is that the events in Sarajevo on Sunday, June 28, 1914, acted as a trigger, starting a chain of events that rapidly led the world to war.

WARNING IGNORED

In *The Great Illusion,* first published in 1909, Norman Angell warned the countries of Europe that war would solve none of their problems:

"It is impossible for one nation to seize by force the wealth or trade of another—to enrich itself by subjugating, or imposing its will by force on another; . . . in short, war, even when victorious, can no longer achieve those aims for which peoples strive."
[From the 1911 edition]

Tragically, for Europe, Angell's words were ignored.

Row after row, these soldiers' gravestones provide a lasting reminder of the many lives lost and dreams unfulfilled.

Important Dates

1871		German **Empire** set up
1879		Germany and Austria-Hungary join in a Dual Alliance
1882		Italy forms a Triple Alliance with Germany and Austria-Hungary
1894		France and Russia join in a Dual Alliance
1904		Britain and France settle their differences in the *Entente* Cordiale
1905–06		Germany backs down from a confrontation over Morocco
1907		Britain and Russia sign an entente, forming the Triple Entente with France
1908		Austria-Hungary takes over Bosnia and Herzegovina. Russia objects but backs down.
1911		Germany backs down from second confrontation over Morocco
1912–13		Serbia gains from two Balkan Wars
1914	June 28	**Assassination** of Archduke Franz Ferdinand
	July 5	Germany's "blank check" to Austria-Hungary
	July 23	Austria-Hungary's **ultimatum** to Serbia
	July 29	Austria-Hungary attacks Serbia
	July 30	Russia prepares for war
	August 1	Germany declares war on Russia
	August 3	Germany declares war on France
	August 4	British Empire declares war on Germany
	November	Turkey joins Germany and Austria-Hungary (the Central Powers)
1915	May	Italy joins Britain, France, and Russia (the **Allies**)
	October	Bulgaria joins the Central Powers
1916	March	Germany declares war on Portugal
	September	Bulgaria attacks Romania
1917	April	United States declares war on Germany
	June	Greece and Brazil join the Allies
	November	**Communists** come to power in Russia
1918		Armistice ends fighting on the Western Front
1919		**Treaty** of Versailles between Germany and the Allies. League of Nations set up. Treaty of St. Germain ends the rule of the Hapsburgs. U.S. Senate rejects the Treaty of Versailles. United States backs away from European affairs.
1920		Treaty of Trianon breaks up Austro-Hungarian Empire. Treaty of Sevres breaks up the Ottoman Empire.
1933		Adolf Hitler comes to power in Germany

Glossary

ally official friend and helper in time of trouble

ambassador someone who represents his or her country in another country

annexation to take possession of a neighboring country or piece of territory

assassination murder committed for political reasons

attrition strategy of wearing down one's enemy in a war

bankrupt in a state of financial ruin

civilian anyone who is not a member of the armed forces

Communist someone who believes that the state, not individual people, should own all important industry, property, and wealth

congress international meeting

conscription when people are forced to join the armed forces

crisis time of danger

empire many countries governed by one nation-state

entente friendly agreement or understanding

entourage group of people responsible for looking after an important person

hereditary inherited by members of the same family

League of Nations organization established in 1919 to try to prevent war, later replaced by the United Nations

minister powerful member of some governments

mobilize to prepare armed forces for war

nation-state country that has its own government

neutral not taking sides during a conflict

pacifist someone who believes war is always wrong

ration to limit food supplies and distribute them equally among people

revolution quick, complete, and permanent change

terrorist person who uses violence and intimidation to achieve a political goal

total war war that involves a country's industry, agriculture, and civilian population, as well as its fighting forces

treaty written agreement between countries

tsar before 1917, an emperor of Russia

ultimatum final demand that must be obeyed to avoid punishment or retaliation

More Books to Read

Dolan, Edward F. *America in World War I*. Brookfield, Conn.: Millbrook Press, Inc., 1996.

Gay, Kathlyn and Martin K. *World War I*. Brookfield, Conn.: Twenty-First Century Books, Inc., 1995.

Ross, Stewart. *Causes & Consequences of World War I*. Austin, Tex: Raintree Steck-Vaughn Pub., 1998.

Index